The Earth

Written by
Cynthia Pratt Nicolson

Illustrated by
Bill Slavin

Kids Can Press Ltd.

For Lidi

Acknowledgments

Writing a book is a great way to learn new things. These scientists have helped me learn about our amazing planet: Mark Halpern, Rosemary Knight, Bob Turner, Catherine Hickson, Paul Hoffman, Verena Tunnicliffe, Garry Rogers, Dieter Wiechert, Ward Chesworth and Brian Hall. Thanks to them all! Also, I am grateful to Peter Russell and his staff at the Earth Sciences Museum of the University of Waterloo for their suggestions on improving the book's final chapter. Of course, any errors that escaped notice are my responsibility.

Many other people have contributed to this book in one way or another. For their support, I would like to thank Deborah Hodge, Linda Bailey, David Gloag, Andrea Mudry Fawcett, Martin Van Nierop, the staff at the West Vancouver Memorial Library and everyone at Kids Can Press. Once again, Val Wyatt has been the perfect editor – tough but fun.

Finally, I want to thank my family. After all, they mean the Earth to me!

First U.S. edition 1997 published by
Kids Can Press Ltd.
85 River Rock Drive, Suite 202
Buffalo, NY 14207

Published in Canada by
Kids Can Press Ltd.
29 Birch Avenue
Toronto, Ontario, Canada
M4V 1E2

Text copyright © 1996 by Cynthia Pratt Nicolson
Illustrations copyright © 1996 by Bill Slavin

Kids Can Press Ltd. acknowledges with appreciation the assistance of the Canada Council and the Ontario Arts Council in the production of this book.

Photo credits

NASA: pages 4, 11, 13, 14
National Oceanic and Atmospheric Administration: page 24
National Oceanic and Atmospheric Administration/National Geophysical Data Center: page 25

Cataloging in Publication Data

Nicolson, Cynthia Pratt
  The earth

(Starting with space)
Includes index.
ISBN 1-55074-314-7

1. Earth — Juvenile literature. I. Slavin, Bill.
II. Title. III. Series.

QB631.4.N53   1996   j525   C95-932370-8

Edited by Valerie Wyatt
Text design by Marie Bartholomew
Page layout and cover design by Esperança Melo
Printed in Hong Kong by Wing King Tong
Co. Ltd.

96 0 9 8 7 6 5 4 3 2

Contents

Earth: Our home in space

You are an Earthling – you live on planet Earth. People have lived on Earth for thousands of years. Plants and animals have been here even longer. But where did Earth itself come from and when? All over the world people have made up stories to explain how Earth began.

Earth stories

The Hurons of North America said a woman fell from the sky when Earth was covered with water. She had no place to stand. So a turtle swam down to the sea floor and scooped up some mud. The woman patted the mud onto the turtle's back to create the first dry land.

In Mexico, the Aztecs told of two gods who built Earth from a sea serpent's body. When the angry monster lashed its tail, an earthquake shook the ground.

If you see a word you don't know, look it up in the glossary on page 39.

The ancient Greeks told stories of Mother Earth, named Gaia, who gave birth to the sea and the sky. Gaia's children were gods and goddesses. They made the winds blow and day follow night.

In China, people said everything began with an egg. Phan Ku, the first living creature, hatched from this egg. He carved the mountains and valleys and plains. When Phan Ku died, his bones became rocks. His blood became rivers and oceans. And the fleas in Phan Ku's hair turned into Earth's first people.

5

How did Earth begin?

Today scientists study the other planets and stars in the universe to find out about Earth's past. Here is what scientists have discovered.

At first, the universe was incredibly hot and everything in it was squeezed close together. Then, about 10 or 15 billion years ago, the universe began to expand and cool. Dust and other particles spread through space. Scientists call this process the Big Bang.

Some of the particles clung together, forming stars and clusters of stars called galaxies. Our Sun was one such star. A flat cloud of dust and gases began to swirl around the Sun. Then, about 4600 million years ago, the cloud separated into lumps. These lumps became the nine major planets, including Earth.

Your usual address

Josephine Blow
456 Celestial Way
Skytown
North America
Earth
The Solar System
The Milky Way Galaxy
The Universe

Earth is your planet.

The solar system is made up of a star (the Sun) and nine planets.

The Milky Way galaxy is made up of about 200 000 million stars.

The universe is made up of 10 000 million galaxies.

TRY IT!
See the Milky Way galaxy

You'll need:
○ a pair of binoculars

1. On a clear night, away from bright city lights, look for a cloudy band of light stretching across the sky.

2. Look at the same part of the sky through the binoculars. Can you see lots of tiny dots? These are stars. There are so many of them that they make a haze of light. The stars are part of the Milky Way galaxy. We live in this galaxy.

Earth

Earth is located in one of the Milky Way's spiral arms.

Who are Earth's neighbors in space?

Earth is one of nine planets in the solar system. It is the third planet away from the Sun.

Is Earth like the other planets?

No. Jupiter, Saturn, Uranus and Neptune are huge balls made mostly of gases. They don't have a solid, rocky crust like Earth.

Mercury, Venus and Mars are solid on the outside like Earth, but you couldn't survive on them. Mercury has long, cold nights and long, hot days. Venus is scorching hot.

Mars is very, very cold. None of these planets has oxygen to breathe or water to drink. (On hotter planets, water evaporates and turns into a gas. On colder planets, water freezes.)

Earth is just right – it is not too hot or too cold. Because of this, Earth is the only planet we know of that has living things.

TRY IT!

Make a miniature solar system

You'll need:
- a golf ball
- a basketball
- a soccer ball
- 2 softballs
- a Ping-Pong ball
- 3 marbles of different sizes

If Earth were the size of a golf ball, the Sun would be as big as an elephant. Here's how big the other planets would be:

Earth

Pluto

Mars

Mercury

Neptune

Uranus

Venus

Saturn

Jupiter

Can you put the balls in the order of the planets in the solar system?

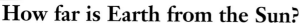

How far is Earth from the Sun?

Earth is about 150 million km (93 million mi.) from the Sun. Sometimes Earth is a bit closer to the Sun than that. At other times it is farther away. Why? Earth's path, or "orbit," around the Sun isn't a perfect circle.

Earth revolves around the Sun once every 365 1/4 days. This gave people the time measurement for one year.

Stick your hand into bright sunshine. It took about eight minutes for the sunlight to travel from the Sun to Earth.

Earth info

Earth is sometimes called the Blue Planet because water covers three-quarters of its surface. Seen from space, the water makes Earth look blue.

Thousands of meteors hurtle toward Earth every year. Most of them burn up in Earth's atmosphere before they hit the ground.

Earth is the fifth largest planet in the solar system, after Jupiter, Saturn, Uranus and Neptune.

Jupiter   Saturn   Uranus   Neptune   Earth

Why does Earth have a moon?
The Moon probably formed from the same cloud of dust that created Earth. It may even be a chunk of Earth that was knocked off by a meteor.

Why does the Moon circle Earth? Earth's invisible pulling force, called gravity, keeps the Moon where it is, orbiting the Earth once every 27 ⅓ days.

Earth, seen from the moon. The Moon is 400 000 km (250 000 mi.) away from Earth. If you bicycled top speed night and day, it would take you three years to cover that distance.

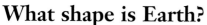

What shape is Earth?

Long ago, people thought Earth was flat – like a plate. They worried about falling off its edge. Today we know that Earth is almost round – like a ball. Measurements taken from satellites show that Earth is 43 km (26.7 mi.) thicker through its middle than it is from pole to pole. Like many people, Earth bulges a little around the waist!

The Sun is so big that if it were a hollow ball, it would take 1 000 000 Earths to fill it.

How big is Earth?

Earth measures about 40 000 km (25 000 mi.) around its middle. You would have to fly in a jet plane for more than 30 hours to travel that far.

Compared to some of the other planets, Earth is tiny. Flying around Jupiter in a jet plane would take 14 days.

What does Earth look like from space?

Only astronauts have been lucky enough to see Earth from space. When Astronaut Neil Armstrong looked back at Earth from the Moon in 1969, he was awestruck by what he saw. Armstrong called Earth "a beautiful jewel in space." Blue water and green lands are draped with veils of white clouds. Imagine peering out the window of a spacecraft and seeing this sight. How would *you* describe Earth?

This photo of Earth was taken by the *Apollo 17* astronauts as they traveled toward the Moon.

Earth, the sky traveler

Are you sitting still? It might feel like it, but you're not. You and Earth are actually hurtling around the Sun at about 106 000 km/h (66 000 m.p.h.). You are breaking the speed limit! Earth's movement around the Sun makes the seasons change. And Earth's turning makes day follow night.

Chasing away the night

Long ago, people thought Earth stayed still and the heavens moved. They made up stories to explain changes in the night sky. Here is how the Vikings explained the movement of the Sun and Moon through the sky.

In the days of trolls and giants, three Viking gods plotted to create a new world. First they made Earth. Then they placed the Sun and Moon in the sky.

But the three gods weren't happy. Nothing moved in their sky! So they put the Sun and Moon into two horse-drawn carts. The Moon was so cold that ice crystals formed in her horses' silvery manes. The Sun made his horses so hot that bellows were needed to cool them.

Trolls who lived on Earth hated the bright light that the Sun and Moon cast in the sky. "Bring back the dark," they grumbled. Two angry trolls came up with a plan. They would turn themselves into wolves and gobble up the Sun and Moon!

The wolves raced into the sky. One chased the Moon and the other took off after the Sun. But the terrified horses pulling the Sun and Moon were too fast for them. Around and around they all raced. As they crossed the sky, night followed day and day followed night. Even now, the Sun and Moon still ride across the sky, fleeing the wolves' snapping jaws.

Why do we have night and day?

We have night and day because Earth turns, like a slowly spinning ball. The turning of the Earth is called rotation. When the side of the Earth where you live faces the Sun, it is daytime. When your part of the Earth is turned away from the Sun, it is dark and you have night.

The rotation of the Earth makes it seem as if the Sun is moving across the sky. The Sun appears to rise in the east in the morning and set in the west at night. But actually it is Earth that is moving, not the Sun.

It is daytime on this half of Earth

... and nighttime on this half of Earth.

I rotate around an imaginary line called an axis. See how my axis is tilted?

Why do we have seasons?

We have winter, spring, summer and fall because Earth is tilted as it circles the Sun. In summer, the place where you live tilts toward the Sun. Sunlight hits your area directly, and the days are long and warm. In winter, your part of Earth tilts away from the Sun. Sunlight hits your area at an angle, and the days are shorter. Because of this, you receive less heat. Brrr!

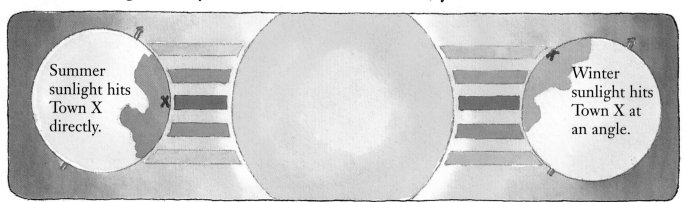

Summer sunlight hits Town X directly.

Winter sunlight hits Town X at an angle.

TRY IT!
Turn day into night

You'll need:
- a large ball (such as a beach-ball or basketball)
- a small piece of masking tape
- a flashlight

1. Imagine that the ball is Earth. Put the masking tape somewhere on the ball to mark where you live.

2. Go into a dark room. Hold the ball as shown.

3. Ask a friend to shine the flashlight directly at the ball. The flashlight is like the Sun.

4. Slowly turn the ball. Watch the taped spot as the ball turns. What happens?

As Earth (your ball) turns, the place where you live (the taped spot) goes through day and night.

Why does the Moon change shape?

The Moon doesn't change shape. It only appears to.

The Moon shines because it reflects light from the Sun. As the Moon circles Earth each month, different parts of the Moon are lit by the Sun. When you look at the Moon, you see only the bright part of the side facing you. Over four weeks, the Moon seems to grow from a thin sliver to a full circle. Then it shrinks to a sliver again. These changes in shape are called the phases of the Moon.

Week one   Week two   Week three   Week four

New Moon   Full Moon

What is an eclipse?

An eclipse of the Sun happens when the Moon crosses in front of the Sun. The Sun's light is blocked out and the sky goes dark.

An eclipse of the Moon happens when the Moon passes into Earth's shadow. Light from the Sun can't get to the Moon, so the Moon looks dark.

Never look directly at the Sun. Ask an adult to help you view an eclipse safely.

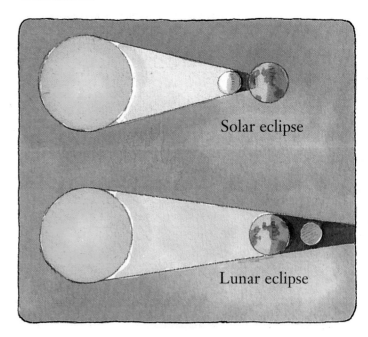

Solar eclipse

Lunar eclipse

TRY IT!

Make an eclipse of the Moon

You'll need:
- a large sheet of black paper
- tape
- a large flashlight
- a large plastic yogurt lid

1. Tape the black paper to a wall.

2. Shine the flashlight (the Sun) onto the paper. Move the flashlight closer to the paper or farther away until you have a clear circle of bright light (the Moon). Ask a friend to hold the flashlight in this position.

3. Move the plastic lid (the Earth) very slowly and steadily across the beam of light. Watch as its shadow nibbles away at the Moon's image on the paper. You have just made an eclipse of the Moon.

Our planet inside and out

Imagine digging a hole down to the very center of the Earth. What would you find? People have always wondered.
In his book *Journey to the Center of the Earth*, Jules Verne wrote about what it might be like deep inside the Earth.

The journey begins

Axel stared into the mouth of the volcano. Then, overcoming his fear, he grabbed a rope and lowered himself down into the darkness.

At the bottom, he met up with his two companions. Together they entered a rock tunnel and started walking. Down and down they walked.

Water flowed from the rock walls. Axel stopped to look around. Then he made a horrible discovery. His two companions were gone!

Axel searched one lava tube after another. Hours passed. His lamp went out and he stumbled along in the dark. Finally, he slid down a steep slope, hit his head on a rock and passed out.

When Axel awoke, he could not believe his eyes. He was on the beach of a vast ocean, deep inside the Earth. Giant mushrooms and ferns grew on the rocky shore. Waves splashed near his feet. Not far away were his two companions.

But what was this? His companions were building a raft to sail across the underground sea. Axel groaned. His inner Earth adventures had just begun.

What is inside Earth?

Since Jules Verne's time, scientists have learned a lot about the inside of our planet. By studying earthquakes, they have found out that Earth is filled with rock and metal, which become hotter and hotter toward Earth's center. Scientists have also discovered that Earth's interior has three main layers: the crust, the mantle and the core.

Earth's crust is like a thin skin of hard rock.

Earth's crust is very thin. If Earth were a tomato, the crust would be its skin.

Earth's mantle contains rock so hot that it is slightly soft, like modeling clay.

Earth's core is even hotter. The outer core contains hot liquid metal.

The inner core is solid metal.

What is Earth's crust like?

Earth's crust is like a jigsaw puzzle made of huge slabs of rock. These slabs, called tectonic plates, float on the melted rock of the mantle below. Ready for a surprise? The tectonic plates are slowly moving. They glide apart, scrape together and smash head-on, causing big changes on Earth's surface. Mountains rise, volcanoes erupt and earthquakes shake the ground.

22

TRY IT!
Make a hard-boiled model of Earth

You'll need:
- a hard-boiled egg
- a kitchen knife

1. Gently tap the egg on a table to make cracks all over its shell.

2. Ask an adult to help you cut the egg in half as shown.

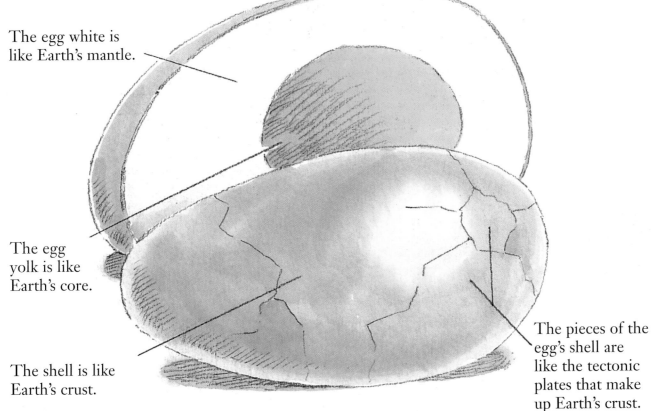

The egg white is like Earth's mantle.

The egg yolk is like Earth's core.

The shell is like Earth's crust.

The pieces of the egg's shell are like the tectonic plates that make up Earth's crust.

How are mountains formed?

Some mountains are formed when two tectonic plates crash together.

Others form when volcanoes spew out lava and ash.

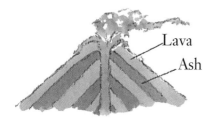

Lava

Ash

Another type of mountain appears when parts of Earth's crust slip up or down.

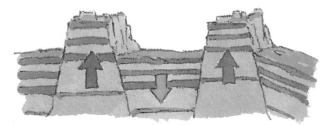

What is on the ocean floor?

If the oceans suddenly dried up, you would see deep canyons, vast plains and tall, jagged peaks. One long mountain chain snakes along the ocean bottom. The mountains in this chain have formed in places where tectonic plates have pulled apart and magma (melted rock) has bubbled up from below.

Earth info

The peak of Mount Everest, in the Himalayas, is Earth's highest point. It is almost 9 km (5.5 mi.) above sea level.

The deepest place on Earth's surface is the Marianas Trench in the south Pacific Ocean. The bottom of the trench is nearly 11 km (7 mi.) below sea level.

If Earth's oceans dried up, this is what you would see.

What causes earthquakes?
When Earth's tectonic plates move around, the rock between them is squeezed, bent and stretched. Sometimes it breaks with a sudden jolt. Vibrations spread in all directions and the ground shakes. It's an earthquake!

Some earthquakes shake the ground so much that nearby buildings fall over.

Why do volcanoes erupt?

Volcanoes erupt when magma spurts up through a crack in Earth's crust. Cracks often occur near the edges of tectonic plates.

The sudden eruption of Mount Vesuvius killed many people in the ancient Roman town of Pompeii. Buried by volcanic ash, Pompeii lay hidden for centuries. Finally, in 1860, workers dug through the hardened ash. They discovered hollow places left by the bodies of the volcano's victims.

TRY IT!
Make your own volcano

You'll need:
- a piece of aluminum foil
  30 cm x 60 cm (12 in. x 24 in.)
- an aluminum pie plate
- a small spoon
- baking powder
- a small bowl
- liquid dish soap
- 125 mL (½ c.) vinegar
- red food coloring

1. Scrunch the sheet of foil into a cone-shaped mountain. Place the mountain in the middle of the pie plate. Make a deep crater in the middle of the cone as shown.

2. Put two spoonfuls of baking powder into the crater.

3. In a small bowl, mix a few drops of dish soap, the vinegar and some red food coloring.

4. Pour this mixture into the cone. What happens?

Real volcanoes spit out lava that is full of air bubbles, much like your homemade lava. But real lava is scorching hot.

What is Earth's atmosphere?

Earth's atmosphere is a covering of gases that surrounds the planet. Some of the gases protect us from the Sun's harmful rays. Others act like an invisible blanket and hold the Sun's warmth close to Earth.

The atmosphere contains the oxygen we need to breathe. It carries water vapor that falls to Earth as rain and snow. Without the atmosphere, people, plants and animals could not survive.

Earth's atmosphere has many layers.

Exosphere

Thermosphere

Mesosphere

Stratosphere

Troposphere

Why do we have weather?

The Sun heats Earth's surface unevenly. This creates huge blobs of warm and cool air in the lowest layer of the atmosphere. Because the warm air is lighter, it tends to rise. Then cool, heavy air rushes in to take its place. Enormous currents of moving air are produced. They swirl around Earth. The result? Breezes, winds, storms and hurricanes.

Rain and snow fall from the sky when moist, warm air suddenly cools and drops its load of water.

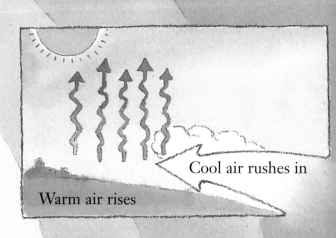

Cool air rushes in

Warm air rises

TRY IT!
Create some currents

You'll need:
- a large, wide-necked clear glass or plastic container
- ice-cold water
- a piece of string
- a small glass bottle
- very hot water
- a small spoon
- blue food coloring

1. Fill the large container about two-thirds full with ice-cold water.

2. Tie the string securely around the neck of the small glass bottle. Make a loop you can hold on to.

3. Ask an adult to fill the small bottle with very hot water. Use the spoon to stir in some blue food coloring.

4. Carefully lower the small bottle to the bottom of the large container. Don't let the small bottle tip.

5. Watch for a few minutes. What happens?

The hot water rises because it is lighter than the cold water around it. The currents you have created are like the air currents in the atmosphere that make Earth's weather.

A living, changing world

In the entire solar system, only planet Earth is a good home for plants, animals and people. How did plants and animals come to live on Earth? And how have they changed Earth?

The story of Raven

The Inuit people tell of a time when Earth was made of soft, wet clay. Raven lived all alone in this damp world. One day, he scooped up some clay in his great black beak and made some dry land. He molded plants and animals, mosses and caribou to live on the land. He shaped whales and fishes and placed them in the sea.

"Welcome to the world," said Raven.

Later, more people jumped out of seed pods. Raven showed them how to hunt and fish. He taught them to make clothes from animal skins and houses from snow.

And that was how the Earth came to be filled with plants and animals – and people.

Then Raven noticed a giant plant. As he watched, one of the plant's seed pods began to wriggle and shake. The pod bulged, first on one side, then on the other. Finally, it split open. Out popped a man!

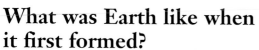

What was Earth like when it first formed?

If you could travel back to the time when Earth was new, you would find a scorching-hot planet. The atmosphere was thick with deadly gases. Earth's surface flowed with melted rock. There was no oxygen to breathe and no solid land to stand on.

Earth slowly cooled. Its crust hardened. Over time, steamy water vapor in the air changed to rain and filled the first oceans. Living things began to grow in the water. Nothing lived on land for millions of years.

Where did the first living things come from?

No one is sure how life on Earth began. But scientists believe life probably started in the soggy clay of early Earth. Chemicals in the clay mixed together. Then they were zapped by lightning or sunlight, or maybe heated by Earth's hot interior. This made them connect in new ways and make living things.

The earliest living things were very simple and small. They may have been something like today's bacteria. Little by little, plants and animals developed from these simple creatures.

All through Earth's long history plants and animals have come and gone as conditions changed.

33

What was Earth like when the dinosaurs lived?

By the time the first dinosaurs appeared, Earth was already more than 4200 million years old. It had changed a lot.

The earliest plants had breathed oxygen into the oceans and atmosphere. So there was oxygen to breathe instead of poisonous gases. Wind and water had worn down some of the rocks to form soil. Some plants and animals had moved from the oceans onto the land.

When the dinosaurs lived, Earth's climate was warmer and wetter than it is now. The dinosaurs waded through swampy forests where ferns grew to the size of trees.

Why did dinosaurs disappear?

Dinosaurs lived on Earth for about 140 million years, then they suddenly disappeared. Some scientists think dinosaurs became extinct when a huge comet or meteor collided with Earth about 65 million years ago. The gigantic crash sent clouds of dust and ash into the sky. These clouds may have blocked out sunlight and made the world too cold for the dinosaurs to survive.

TRY IT!
Stretch out a time line

You'll need:
- masking tape
- a pen
- a long tape measure
- a large ball of yarn
- a huge open space such as a school yard

1. Put a piece of masking tape at the end of the yarn as shown to make a label. Write "Today" on this label.

TODAY

2. Unroll 65 cm (26 in.) of yarn to show the 65 million years since the dinosaurs disappeared. Put another masking tape label at this spot and write on it "65 million years ago: dinosaurs disappeared."

3. Continue to unroll and measure the yarn. Put tape labels at these distances:

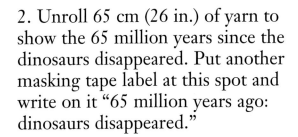

46 m (151 ft.)
4600 million years ago: Earth began

35 m (115 ft.)
3500 million years ago: first living things appeared

4 m (13 ft.)
400 million years ago: plants and animals moved onto land

65 cm (26 in.)
65 million years ago: dinosaurs disappeared

2 m (78 in.)
200 million years ago: dinosaurs appeared

Today

Your time line to the beginning of Earth stretches across a school yard. Yet you can easily reach your arms from "Today" back to the early years of the dinosaurs. And all of human history can be covered with the tip of your little finger.

How is Earth changing?

Over millions of years our planet has changed in many ways. Once Earth had only one supercontinent. Now it has seven continents – Europe, Asia, Australia, Antarctica, North America, South America and Africa. Even the land itself has changed. New mountains have been pushed up. Old mountains have been worn down by wind and ice and water. The wearing down of land is called erosion.

Earth's climate, which was so warm for the dinosaurs, has cooled. At certain times ice has covered much of the land. Then Earth has warmed up again.

Many kinds of plants and animals have appeared and disappeared. During the last 100 000 years, people have spread all over Earth. And with people have come other changes, such as cities and roads and pollution.

Over time, erosion will wear down the jagged new mountains behind me until they look like these rounded old mountains.

What is pollution?

Pollution is anything harmful that people put into the land, air or water. Some pollution from cars and factories rises into the atmosphere. It can eat holes in the layers of gases that protect Earth from the Sun's harmful rays. Or it can make a very thick blanket of gases around Earth that keeps in too much of the Sun's heat. Pollution may change Earth's climate. And big changes may make it hard for some living things to survive.

Why is Earth a good place to live?

Earth is a special planet. It has just the right combination of warmth, sunlight, water and air for people, plants and animals. Its atmosphere provides us with the oxygen we need to breathe and protects us from most of the Sun's unhealthy rays. As far as we know, Earth is the only planet that isn't too hot or too cold, too dry or too frozen, for the survival of living things.

Astronaut Jim Lovell was part of the first space crew to circle the Moon. When he looked back at Earth, he said, "The Earth from here is a grand oasis in the great vastness of space."

37

Why study Earth?

Research about Earth's atmosphere helps us decide how to control pollution. Probing the planet's crust lets us find valuable resources, such as oil and minerals. Studying Earth's crust and interior warns us of earthquake areas and volcanic eruptions.

Earth is our home. And it is home to more and more people every year. We Earthlings need to understand our planet so that we can take good care of it.

Glossary

atmosphere: a layer of gases surrounding Earth

axis: an imaginary line running through Earth from the North Pole to the South Pole

continent: a major land mass

core: the center part of Earth

crust: the outer layer of Earth

earthquake: a sudden jolt that shakes the ground

eclipse: a darkening of the Sun or Moon

galaxy: a large group of stars

gravity: an invisible pulling force

lava: melted rock above ground, usually coming from volcanoes

lunar: of the Moon

magma: melted rock inside Earth

mantle: Earth's middle layer

meteor: a piece of space rock that falls through Earth's atmosphere

Milky Way: the galaxy Earth is in

orbit: the path of a planet or moon around another heavenly body

oxygen: a gas we need to breathe

revolution: Earth's motion around the Sun

rotation: Earth's turning on its axis

solar: of the Sun

solar system: the Sun and nine planets around it

tectonic plates: slabs of Earth's crust

volcano: a place where magma spurts through Earth's crust

Index